A SHORT E-BOOK

Marketing Funnels

A Journey Through Time and Their Demise

BY: ANDREW MOUNIER

About the Author

Meet Andrew Mounier, a highly respected marketing expert with nearly two decades of experience consulting and working with over 50 leading brands. Andrew has served in various positions, including VP of Marketing for Orbit, VP of Growth Marketing for Agorapulse, and Director of Marketing for Sumo.com and Process Street. His expertise in the industry has earned him a place on the FastCompany Executive Board, and he's a regular contributor to major media outlets like FastCompany and Forbes.

Andrew is a master of turning ordinary marketing into something extraordinary. He's experimented with various strategies, from the bullseye framework and inbound SEO optimization to guerrilla marketing tactics that defy convention, helping him achieve remarkable results. He's served as CMO for a $500 million revenue organization, built multiple in-house marketing teams from scratch, and operates a content marketing and growth marketing consulting firm with clients on the Fortune 500 and 1000.

But what truly sets Andrew apart is his unwavering commitment to challenging the status quo. As a marketing expert, he relentlessly combines and refines ideas to achieve exponential growth for his clients. As the founder of WordSmiths, Inc., he is dedicated to helping businesses achieve their full potential.

When he's not helping businesses grow, Andrew is hosting his hit podcast Le Crieriers, where he uncovers the untold stories of modern-day street criers, revealing the passion, purpose, and strategies behind today's most innovative tech brands.

He's also an avid traveler who loves to explore the world with his partner, Lili, and their new addition to the pack, Twilla.

Want to unleash your business's full potential? Contact Andrew at andrew@wordsmithsinc.com and let him help you create something extraordinary.

WWW.WORDSMITHSINC.COM

Contents

Introduction:

Once upon a time, in a land not so far, far away, there was a cornerstone of marketing strategy known as the sales funnel. For over a century, marketers had relied on this funnel to attract and retain customers. However, the world was constantly evolving, and the funnel was no longer the most effective way to stay ahead of the competition.

As enchanting as the idea of a "sales funnel" may seem, the reality is that it is no longer the most effective way to attract and retain customers. In today's ever-evolving business landscape, the traditional sales funnel has become obsolete. The world of marketing has moved beyond the funnel and is now embracing modern strategies and frameworks that are better suited for the fast-paced digital age we live in.

In this ebook, we'll take a journey through time to understand the rise and fall of the sales funnel and explore the innovative marketing approaches that B2B companies can use to stay ahead of the competition.

In this section, we will briefly go over each chapter of the book and then we will do a deeper dive into the strengths and weaknesses of each framework.

AIDA Funnel Model - "Elmo's Funnel":

The AIDA model (Attention, Interest, Desire, Action) is a classic funnel model that is still widely used today. We'll dive into the details of each stage and explore how B2B companies can optimize their marketing efforts at each step of the funnel.

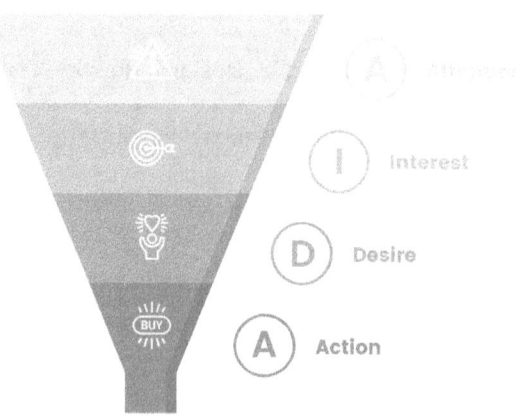

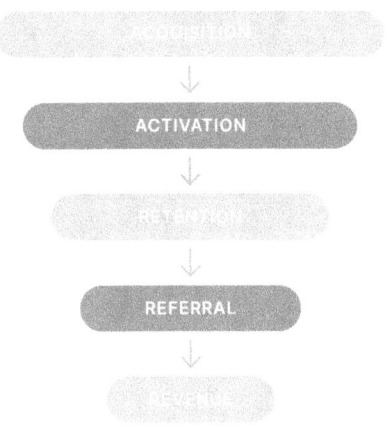

AAARR (Pirate Funnel) Funnel Framework:

The AAARR funnel (Awareness, Activation, Revenue, Retention) is a newer funnel framework that is gaining popularity among B2B companies. We'll explore each stage of the funnel and provide examples of how B2B companies can apply the framework to their marketing strategy.

Growth Loops:

Growth loops are a circular process where the end goal is to create a self-sustaining system that continuously attracts and retains customers. We'll explore the key components of growth loops and provide examples of successful B2B companies that have utilized this strategy.

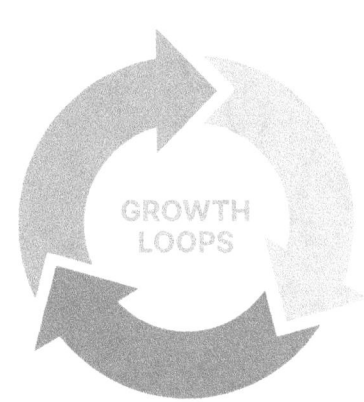

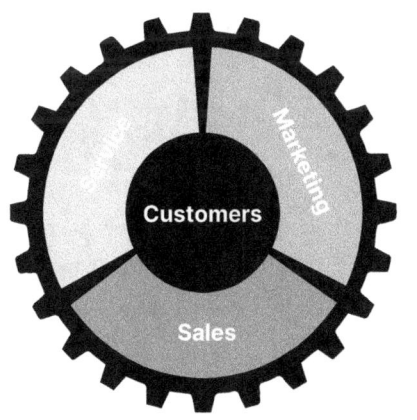

Flywheels:

Flywheels are similar to growth loops, but with a focus on accelerating growth. We'll explore the concept of flywheels and how B2B companies can use this framework to drive exponential growth.

Bowtie/Data Funnel:

The customer purchase funnel doesn't stop after a sale is closed. Once a prospect turns into a customer, there are multiple opportunities to upsell, expand, and create recurring revenue. We'll explore the bowtie/data funnel model and how B2B companies can use this framework to maximize revenue and customer lifetime value.

The Data Model

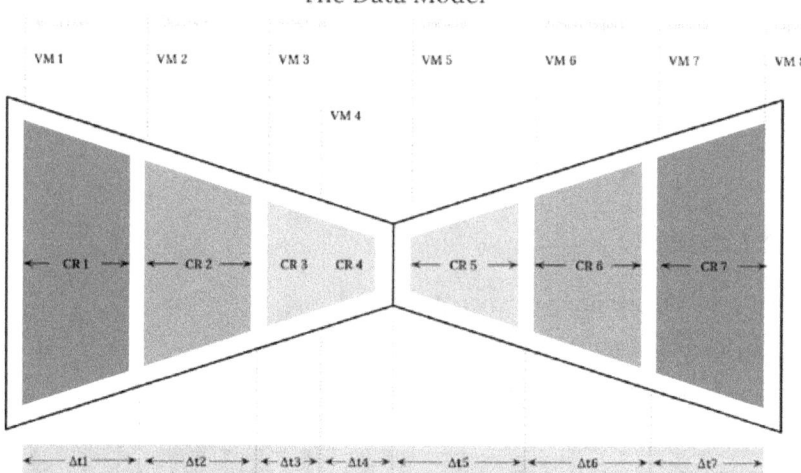

Business Stage:

Understanding your business stage is crucial for determining what strategy you should utilize. We'll explore the different business stages (product-market fit, go-to-market fit, and scale-up) and provide examples of successful B2B companies that have used each strategy.

Summary:

The sales funnel may be broken, but there are plenty of modern marketing strategies and frameworks that B2B companies can use to stay ahead of the curve. We hope this ebook has provided you with valuable insights and inspiration for your next marketing campaign. Remember, the key to success is to continuously adapt and evolve your marketing strategy to meet the needs of your customers.

Chapter 1: AIDA Funnel Model - "Elmo's Funnel":

The AIDA Funnel Model, also known as "Elmo's Funnel," is one of the oldest and most widely used marketing models in the world (Polk, 2018). Developed by E. St. Elmo Lewis in 1898, the model is based on four stages: Attention, Interest, Desire, and Action (Banerjee, 2022).

E. St. Elmo Lewis was an American advertising executive who lived in the late 19th and early 20th centuries. At the time, Lewis was working as an advertising copywriter and was tasked with creating ads that could generate more sales for his clients (does that sound familiar?). However, he quickly realized that the traditional approach to advertising, which focused solely on promoting the features and benefits of a product, was not enough to convince potential customers to make a purchase.

It is amazing that the debate on how to best position a product is still going on. Most of the copy you see on B2B websites focuses purely on product benefits. How is this still happening?

Lewis believed that there was a psychological journey that potential customers went through before making a purchase decision. He theorized that marketers could guide customers through this journey by following a series of steps, starting with grabbing their attention, generating interest in the product, creating a desire to own it, and ultimately inspiring them to take action and make a purchase.

To help explain this concept, Lewis developed the AIDA model. His model proved to be highly effective and soon became a cornerstone of marketing strategy, with companies around the world utilizing it to guide their customers through the buying process.

Lewis's impact on the world of marketing has been long-lasting and significant, and his work laid the foundation for many of the modern marketing practices that are still used today.
In this chapter, we'll dive into each stage of the funnel and explore how companies can optimize their marketing efforts at each step.

Attention:

The first stage of the funnel is Attention. This is where you need to grab the attention of your target audience and make them aware of your product or service (Chakraborti,2020). B2B-companies can optimize their marketing efforts in this stage by:

- **Defining their target audience:** To grab the attention of your target audience, you need to know who they are and what they're interested in. Defining your target audience is the first step in creating effective marketing campaigns.

- **Creating compelling content:** Whether it's a blog post, video, or social media ad, your content needs to be compelling enough to grab the attention of your target audience.

- **Leveraging social media:** Social media is a powerful tool for reaching a large audience quickly. By using social media platforms like LinkedIn, Twitter, and Facebook, B2B companies can increase their brand visibility and attract potential customers.

Interest:

The second stage of the funnel is Interest. Once you've grabbed the attention of your target audience, you need to keep them interested in your product or service (Copley, 2015). B2B companies can optimize their marketing efforts in this stage by:

- **Offering value:** Your content needs to provide value to your target audience. This could be in the form of educational content, thought leadership pieces, or case studies.

- **Focusing on benefits:** Rather than focusing solely on features, B2B companies should focus on the benefits of their product or service. This will help potential customers understand how your product or service can help them solve a problem or achieve a goal.

- **Building trust:** Building trust is crucial for keeping potential customers interested in your product or service. This can be achieved by providing social proof, such as customer testimonials, and by being transparent about your business practices.

Desire:

The third stage of the funnel is Desire. At this stage, you need to create a sense of desire for your product or service (Ginoski, 2019). B2B companies can optimize their marketing efforts in this stage by:

- **Showing the value proposition:** By demonstrating the value proposition of your product or service, you can create a sense of desire among potential customers. This could be done through case studies, ROI calculations, or product demos.

- **Addressing objections:** Potential customers may have objections to your product or service. By addressing these objections head-on, you can help alleviate any concerns and create a greater sense of desire.

- **Creating urgency:** Creating a sense of urgency can help drive potential customers to take action. This could be done through limited-time offers, countdown timers, or scarcity tactics.

Action:

The final stage of the funnel is Action. At this stage, you need to motivate potential customers to take action and make a purchase (TOUHILL, 2022). B2B companies can optimize their marketing efforts in this stage by:

- **Providing a clear call-to-action:** Your call-to-action should be clear and concise, letting potential customers know exactly what they need to do to make a purchase.

- **Offering incentives:** Offering incentives, such as discounts or free trials, can help motivate potential customers to take action.

- **Making the process easy:** The purchasing process should be as easy and streamlined as possible (Harvard Business Review)

A "perfect" example of an AIDA Funnel

Imagine you run a B2B software company and are looking to generate leads for your product. You create an ad campaign that targets people in your industry and highlights the key benefits of your software.

- **Attention:** You catch the attention of potential customers by using eye-catching graphics and headline in your ad (Distel, 2022). You might also use retargeting to show the ad to people who have visited your website before.

- **Interest:** Once someone clicks on the ad, you pique their interest by providing more information about your software (Jerath, 2014), such as its features, ease of use, and the problems it solves. This might be done through a landing page that goes into detail about the product.

- **Desire:** As you educate the potential customer about your software, you want to create a sense of desire for your product. This could be achieved by showcasing customer success stories or offering a free trial or demo that allows them to see the benefits of your software firsthand.

- **Action:** Finally, you want to encourage the potential customer to take action and become a lead. This could be achieved by including a call-to-action in your ad or on your landing page, such as "Sign up for a free trial" or "Contact us for more information."

By following the AIDA model, you have now successfully taken a potential customer from first discovering your product to becoming a lead for your business.

Wouldn't it be nice if life was really this easy and everyone went down a simple funnel?

Unfortunately, life is messy. The AIDA model is a great general concept but it has strengths and weaknesses, which are important to understand for any B2B company looking to optimize its marketing efforts.

Strengths:

- **Simplicity:** The AIDA model is a simple and straightforward model that is easy to understand and apply. It provides a clear roadmap for how to move prospects through the funnel toward a purchase.

- **Customer-focused:** The model is centered around the customer's journey and their needs and desires. It starts by capturing their attention and ends with them taking action.

- **Applicable to a wide range of industries:** The AIDA model is applicable to almost any industry, making it a versatile and valuable tool for B2B marketers.

- **Emphasizes the importance of storytelling:** The model highlights the importance of creating a compelling story that captures the customer's attention and builds desire.

Weaknesses:

- **Oversimplification:** The model can be oversimplified, and in reality, the customer journey is often more complex than just the four stages explained above.

- **Limited focus on customer retention:** The model's focus is mainly on acquiring new customers, and it doesn't take into account the importance of customer retention and upselling (Ullal, & Hawaldar, 2018).

- **Ignores customer feedback:** The model assumes that the customer's desire will naturally lead to action, but it doesn't take into account the importance of customer feedback in guiding marketing efforts.

- **Doesn't address post-purchase experience:** The model doesn't address the post-purchase experience, which can be a critical factor in creating customer loyalty and advocacy.

Understanding the strengths and weaknesses of the AIDA model is important for B2B companies looking to optimize their marketing efforts. While the model provides a useful framework, it should be used in conjunction with other models and customer feedback to create a comprehensive marketing strategy.

Chapter 2: AAARR (Pirate Funnel) Funnel Framework:

The AAARR funnel, also known as the Pirate Funnel, is a modern funnel framework that was popularized by Dave McClure, a prominent entrepreneur and investor in the Silicon Valley startup scene (Ratcliffe, 2017). McClure first introduced the AAARR framework in 2007 as part of a presentation on startup metrics, where he identified the five key stages of the customer journey that startups should focus on to drive growth. These stages include Awareness, Acquisition, Activation, Revenue, and Retention.

The Pirate Funnel gets its name from the acronym AAARR, which sounds like a pirate's battle cry. It is designed to help startups prioritize their marketing efforts by identifying the key metrics that matter at each stage of the funnel.

Background and Use Case of the AAARR (Pirate Funnel) Funnel Framework

The Pirate Funnel was created as a response to the limitations of the traditional sales funnel. The traditional sales funnel is linear and one-directional and assumes that the customer journey ends with a sale. The Pirate Funnel, on the other hand, is circular and iterative and recognizes that the customer journey continues beyond a sale.

The AAARR framework is designed to help companies optimize their marketing and growth strategies at each stage of the customer journey (Van Gasteren, 2022). Here is a breakdown of each stage:

- **Acquisition:** This is the first stage of the funnel, where you acquire new customers (Lieberman, 2019). This can be done through various marketing channels, such as social media, search engine marketing, content marketing, and paid advertising.

- **Activation:** Once you've acquired a customer, the next step is to activate them. Activation refers to the point where the customer takes a desired action, such as signing up for a free trial or making their first purchase.

- **Retention:** The third stage of the funnel is retention. This stage is all about keeping the customer engaged and using your product or service. The goal is to retain the customer for as long as possible, by providing value and building a relationship with them (Team, 2023).

- **Referral:** The fourth stage of the funnel is referral. This stage is all about turning your existing customers into advocates for your brand. The goal is to encourage your customers to refer their friends and family to your product or service.

- **Revenue:** The final stage of the funnel is revenue. This stage is all about maximizing the value of your current customer base. The goal is to increase revenue by upselling, cross-selling, and creating new products or services that meet the needs of your customers.

Let's now take this framework and apply it to a real-world scenario.

B2B Business Example:

ABC Software is a B2B software company that provides project management software for small and medium-sized businesses. Here's how they could apply the AAARR method:

- **Awareness:** ABC Software could use targeted online ads and social media campaigns to generate awareness about their software among small and medium-sized business owners and managers.

- **Acquisition:** To acquire new customers, ABC Software could offer a free trial or a demo of their software, and encourage sign-ups through email marketing and landing pages.

- **Activation:** After a customer signs up, ABC Software could provide personalized onboarding and support to ensure that they become active and loyal users of their software.

- **Revenue:** To increase revenue, ABC Software could offer premium plans with more features and functionality, as well as value-added services such as training and support.

- **Retention:** ABC Software could engage with their customers through email and social media, release regular product updates, and offer ongoing customer support to encourage retention and turn customers into brand advocates.

B2C Business Example:

XYZ Beauty is a B2C cosmetics company that sells high-quality, natural beauty products. Here's how they could apply the AAARR method:

- **Awareness:** XYZ Beauty could use social media advertising and influencer marketing to generate brand awareness among young women interested in natural beauty products.

- **Acquisition:** To acquire new customers, XYZ Beauty could offer a discount or a free sample of their products through email marketing and landing pages.

- **Activation:** After a customer makes a purchase, XYZ Beauty could provide personalized product recommendations and encourage customers to share their experiences with their friends and family.

- **Revenue:** To increase revenue, XYZ Beauty could offer subscription boxes with monthly product deliveries, as well as upsell and cross-sell opportunities for related beauty products.

- **Retention:** XYZ Beauty could provide excellent customer service, engage with customers through email and social media, and offer loyalty programs to encourage retention and turn customers into brand advocates.

In both examples, the AAARR method provides a clear framework for each business to optimize its marketing efforts and improve their customer journey, ultimately leading to increased growth and success.

A "perfect" example of an AIDA Funnel

Strengths:

- The Pirate Funnel is a holistic and iterative framework that recognizes the importance of the customer journey beyond the sale.

- The framework is adaptable and can be tailored to fit the specific needs of different businesses and industries.

- The Pirate Funnel is data-driven, which makes it easy to track and measure the success of your marketing and growth efforts.

- The framework emphasizes the importance of customer retention and referral, which can lead to long-term growth and success.

Weaknesses:

- The Pirate Funnel is primarily designed for B2C companies and may not be as applicable to B2B companies.

- The framework can be complex and may require significant resources and expertise to implement effectively.

- The Pirate Funnel is focused on growth and acquisition, which may lead to a short-term mindset and neglect of long-term sustainability.

Chapter 3: Growth Loops

Growth loops are a marketing framework that focuses on the ongoing cycle of acquiring, activating, and retaining customers. It differs from traditional funnel models in that it seeks to create a self-sustaining system that drives growth organically through customer referrals and retention (Growth Loops). The framework was popularized by Brian Balfour, a growth expert and former VP of Growth at HubSpot. Growth loops are particularly effective for companies with high customer lifetime value, as they allow for the constant acquisition of new customers while retaining existing ones. You can learn more about Growth Loops at: https://www.reforge.com/blog/growth-loops.

I have always found real-life examples as the best way to learn. Below are 11 examples that quickly break down the growth loops of some of the world's most successful companies.

- **Airbnb:** Airbnb is a prime example of a company that has successfully used growth loops to drive exponential growth. When a host lists their property on Airbnb, they become a natural advocate for the platform and are incentivized to invite their friends and family to also become hosts. This leads to a positive feedback loop where more hosts attract more guests, which in turn attracts more hosts, and so on. Airbnb also uses personalized recommendations and targeted messaging to engage and retain customers, further fueling the growth loop.

- **Dropbox:** Dropbox is another company that has effectively utilized growth loops to drive rapid growth. When a user signs up for Dropbox, they are encouraged to invite their friends and colleagues to also sign up. As more people sign up and use Dropbox, they generate more referrals, which leads to more sign-ups, and so on. Dropbox also uses targeted content and personalized experiences to engage users and encourage retention, driving further growth.

   Peloton: Peloton is a fitness company that has used growth loops to become one of the fastest-growing companies in the world.

When a user purchases a Peloton bike, they become part of a community of Peloton riders who can compete with and support each other through the platform. This community aspect of the Peloton experience leads to a positive feedback loop where more riders attract more riders, which in turn leads to increased engagement, retention, and revenue. Peloton also uses personalized content and targeted marketing to engage and retain customers, further fueling the growth loop.

- **Slack:** Slack is a workplace communication platform that has become one of the most popular tools for teams to communicate and collaborate. When a team signs up for Slack, they become advocates for the platform and are incentivized to invite other teams to also sign up. This leads to a positive feedback loop where more teams attract more teams, which in turn leads to increased engagement, retention, and revenue. Slack also uses personalized recommendations and targeted content to engage and retain customers, further fueling the growth loop.

- **Uber:** Uber is a ride-sharing platform that has revolutionized the transportation industry. When a user signs up for Uber, they become an advocate for the platform and are incentivized to invite their friends and family to also sign up. This leads to a positive feedback loop where more riders attract more riders, which in turn attracts more drivers, leading to increased engagement, retention, and revenue. Uber also uses personalized content and targeted marketing to engage and retain customers, further fueling the growth loop.

- **Headspace:** Headspace is a meditation and mindfulness app that has become increasingly popular in recent years. When a user signs up for Headspace, they become part of a community of users who can support and encourage each other through the platform. This community aspect of the Headspace experience leads to a positive feedback loop where more users attract more users, which in turn leads to increased engagement, retention, and revenue. Headspace also uses personalized content and targeted marketing to engage and retain customers, further fueling the growth loop.

- **HubSpot:** HubSpot is an inbound marketing and sales platform that provides software, tools, and services to help businesses attract, engage, and delight customers. HubSpot uses a growth loop by offering free tools and content that help businesses improve their marketing and sales efforts. When businesses use these free tools, they become advocates for HubSpot and are incentivized to invite their colleagues and peers to also use the platform. This leads to a positive feedback loop where more businesses attract more businesses, which in turn leads to increased engagement, retention, and revenue.

- **Duolingo:** Duolingo is a language-learning platform that has become one of the most popular language apps in the world. Duolingo uses a growth loop by gamifying the language-learning experience and encouraging users to practice regularly. When users practice regularly and improve their language skills, they become advocates for the platform and are incentivized to invite their friends and family to also use the app. This leads to a positive feedback loop where more users attract more users, which in turn leads to increased engagement, retention, and revenue.

- **Canva:** Canva is a graphic design platform that provides users with tools and templates to create professional-looking designs without the need for extensive design skills. Canva uses a growth loop by providing free templates and tools that users can use to create designs. When users create designs and share them on social media, they become advocates for the platform and are incentivized to invite their friends and colleagues to also use the platform. This leads to a positive feedback loop where more users attract more users, which in turn leads to increased engagement, retention, and revenue.

- **TikTok:** TikTok is a social media platform that allows users to create and share short videos. TikTok uses a growth loop by encouraging users to create and share content with their followers. When users create and share engaging content, they become advocates for the platform and are incentivized to invite their friends and followers to also use TikTok. This leads to a positive feedback loop where more users attract more users, which in turn leads to increased engagement, retention, and revenue.

- **Calm:** Calm is a meditation and sleep app that helps users relax and reduce stress. Calm uses a growth loop by providing users with personalized content and recommendations based on their interests and preferences. When users engage with the personalized content and improve their mental health, they become advocates for the platform and are incentivized to invite their friends and family to also use the Calm app. This leads to a positive feedback loop where more users attract more users, which in turn leads to increased engagement, retention, and revenue.

Strengths:

- **Customer-centric:** Growth loops prioritize the customer experience and create a positive feedback loop that encourages customer referrals and retention.

- **Scalable:** Unlike traditional funnel models, growth loops can scale exponentially as more customers are acquired and retained.

- **Low customer acquisition costs:** With growth loops, the majority of customer acquisition comes from referrals, which are often free or low cost.

Weaknesses

- **Not suitable for all businesses:** Growth loops work best for companies with high customer lifetime value, as the cycle of acquiring, activating, and retaining customers may not be as effective for businesses with low customer lifetime value

- **Longer time frame:** Growth loops can take longer to show results compared to traditional funnel models, as they rely on organic growth through customer referrals and retention.

Summary

Growth loops offer a customer-centric approach to marketing that prioritizes the ongoing cycle of acquiring, activating, and retaining customers. While they may not be suitable for all businesses, growth loops can be highly effective for companies with high customer lifetime value. By incentivizing referrals and retention, growth loops can create a self-sustaining system that drives organic growth and scalability.

Chapter 4: The Flywheel Model

The flywheel model first made its appearance in Jim Collins' influential book "Good to Great," where it served to illustrate the concept of sustainable growth (Halligan, 2018). Envisioned as a self-sustaining system, the flywheel gains momentum as it goes through an ongoing loop of inputs, actions, and outcomes. When applied to the business world, the flywheel model facilitates growth by focusing on customer satisfaction and fostering customer loyalty.

Below we will go into a few fictional examples of the flywheel being used on the B2B and B2C sides.

- **B2B Example: SaaS Company**

  A SaaS company uses the Flywheel Method to encourage customer success and advocacy. They focus on:

  - **Onboarding:** Providing seamless onboarding and personalized training to ensure customers can quickly benefit from the product.

  - **Customer Success:** Assigning dedicated customer success managers to address concerns, offer best practices, and maximize product value.

    Advocacy: Encouraging satisfied customers to leave reviews, provide testimonials, and refer new clients to fuel the company's growth.

- **B2B Example: Consulting Firm**

  A management consulting firm implements the Flywheel Method by offering valuable content, fostering relationships, and building a community:

  - **Content Marketing:** Sharing insightful articles, case studies, and webinars to demonstrate expertise and attract clients.

  - **Networking:** Engaging in industry events and conferences to build relationships and stay top-of-mind.

- **Networking:** Engaging in industry events and conferences to build relationships and stay top-of-mind.

- **Community:** Creating a members-only group or forum for clients to share experiences, ask questions, and learn from each other, driving loyalty and referrals.

B2C Example: E-commerce Store

An e-commerce store uses the Flywheel Method to enhance the customer experience and turn buyers into brand advocates:

- **Personalization:** Offering personalized product recommendations, tailored discounts, and targeted marketing messages.

- **Customer Support:** Providing exceptional customer service through chatbots, social media, and email to solve issues promptly.

- **Loyalty Program:** Implementing a rewards system to incentivize repeat purchases, referrals, and social media shares.

B2C Example: Fitness Studio

A fitness studio embraces the Flywheel Method by creating a supportive community and nurturing customer relationships:

- **Experiences:** Hosting in-person and virtual classes, workshops, and social events to engage customers and foster connections.

- **Communication:** Utilizing email newsletters, social media, and in-app messages to share studio updates, promotions, and member spotlights.

- **Ambassador Program:** Encouraging loyal customers to become brand ambassadors, promoting the studio in exchange for exclusive perks and benefits.

Strengths of the Flywheel Model:

- **Customer-Centric:** The flywheel model places the customer at the center of the growth strategy, which can help businesses create a better experience for their customers.

- **Sustainable Growth:** By creating a self-sustaining system, the flywheel model can help businesses achieve long-term growth.

- **Collaboration:** The flywheel model encourages collaboration across departments, which can help businesses break down silos and improve communication.

Weaknesses of the Flywheel Model:

- **Initial Investment:** The flywheel model requires significant initial investment in creating a positive customer experience, which may not be feasible for all businesses.

- **Slow Growth:** The flywheel model may take longer to generate significant results compared to other growth strategies.

- **Limited Scope:** The flywheel model focuses on generating repeat business and may not be as effective in attracting new customers.

Summary:

In this chapter of "The Funnel is Broken," we dove into the flywheel model, a customer-centric approach to growth. The focus here is on fostering positive customer experiences and nurturing repeat business. While it may require a considerable initial investment, the flywheel model paves the way for long-term, sustainable growth.

One of the key benefits of the flywheel model is its ability to facilitate collaboration and communication across departments, breaking down barriers and enhancing internal processes.

Keep in mind, however, that the flywheel model might take more time to produce significant results compared to other strategies, and its effectiveness in attracting new customers could be less pronounced. Nonetheless, the flywheel model emphasizes the importance of putting people at the core of your marketing strategy.

Chapter 5: Difference Between Growth Loops & Flywheels

If you are like me you might feel like Growth Loops and Flywheels are pretty much the same thing. But, there is actually a pretty big difference.

In the most simple terms possible: Growth loops prioritize creating a self-sustaining system where each stage of the customer journey generates more value for the customer and the business, leading to increased engagement and retention over time.

Flywheels, on the other hand, prioritize creating a strong initial spark that can ignite a rapid acceleration of growth, which is often driven by a surge of new customer acquisitions (Nizami, 2019).

Deeper Dive

A growth loop is a circular process where each stage of the customer journey feeds into the next, ultimately driving continuous growth (Redien-Collot, 2022). The focus is on creating a positive feedback loop where each customer touchpoint generates more value for the customer and the business, leading to increased engagement, retention, and revenue.

On the other hand, a flywheel is a circular process where the goal is to create momentum and accelerate growth. The focus is on creating a self-sustaining system that continuously attracts and retains customers, ultimately driving exponential growth.

One of the key differences between flywheels and growth loops is the level of emphasis on the initial stages of the customer journey. With growth loops, the focus is on creating a positive feedback loop that leads to sustainable growth over time. With flywheels, the focus is on creating a strong initial spark that can ignite a rapid acceleration of growth.

Another difference is the level of emphasis on customer retention. While both frameworks prioritize customer retention, growth loops place a greater emphasis on retention as a key driver of growth. With growth loops, the goal is to create a self-sustaining system where each stage of the customer journey generates more value for the customer and the business, leading to increased engagement and retention over time.

In contrast, flywheels place a greater emphasis on customer acquisition as a key driver of business growth. With flywheels, the goal is to create a strong initial spark that can ignite a rapid acceleration of growth, which is often driven by a big surge of new customer acquisitions.

Chapter 6: Winning by Design's Bowtie / Data Funnel

In recent years, the Bowtie / Data Funnel has become an increasingly popular model for B2B companies to optimize their sales and marketing efforts. Developed by Winning by Design, a sales consultancy firm, the Bowtie model is an excellent way to understand the sales process from the customer's point of view.

Background and Use Case:

The Bowtie / Data Funnel is a hybrid model that combines elements of the traditional sales funnel and the customer journey. The model provides a visual representation of how prospects move through the sales process and how customer engagement can lead to further opportunities. The Bowtie model includes two funnels - one for the buyer journey and one for the customer journey. The buyer funnel shows how prospects move from awareness to purchase, while the customer funnel shows how companies can upsell, expand, and create recurring revenue after the sale.

The Bowtie model allows companies to understand their customers' needs, pain points, and motivations. This model can help companies optimize their sales and marketing efforts by providing a clear picture of how their customers make purchasing decisions.

To help illustrate how the bowtie model can be effectively applied in both B2B and B2C contexts, let's take a look at two examples showcasing how businesses can leverage this strategy to drive growth and customer satisfaction.

B2B Example - A SaaS Company:

A SaaS company specializing in project management software could employ the bowtie model to not only acquire new customers but also retain and expand their relationship with existing clients.

- **Acquisition:** Attract potential customers through targeted content marketing, webinars, and paid advertising.

- **Conversion:** Offer free trials and personalized demos to showcase the software's value and features.

- **Expansion:** Once a client is onboard, offer training and support to ensure they utilize the software to its fullest potential.

- **Retention:** Regularly check in with clients, provide updates, and gather feedback to maintain satisfaction and improve the product.

Advocacy: Encourage satisfied clients to share their experiences and refer new clients, offering incentives such as discounts or exclusive features.

B2C Example - An Online Clothing Retailer:

An online clothing retailer could use the bowtie model to attract new customers, retain their existing customer base, and encourage brand loyalty.

- **Acquisition:** Utilize social media advertising, influencers, and SEO to drive traffic to their website.

- **Conversion:** Offer first-time purchase discounts, free shipping, and an easy-to-navigate website to encourage sales.

- **Expansion:** Send personalized recommendations based on purchase history, and introduce a loyalty program for repeat customers.

- **Retention:** Provide excellent customer service, hassle-free returns, and consistent communication through newsletters and social media.

- **Acquisition:** Utilize social media advertising, influencers, and SEO to drive traffic to their website.

- **Conversion:** Offer first-time purchase discounts, free shipping, and an easy-to-navigate website to encourage sales.

- **Expansion:** Send personalized recommendations based on purchase history, and introduce a loyalty program for repeat customers.

- **Retention:** Provide excellent customer service, hassle-free returns, and consistent communication through newsletters and social media.

Strengths & Weaknesses

In our journey to better understand the Bowtie/Data Funnel model, it's crucial to recognize both its strengths and weaknesses. By evaluating the advantages and potential challenges of this approach, you can make a more informed decision about whether it's the right fit for your organization. In this section, we'll explore the key strengths and weaknesses of the Bowtie/Data Funnel model to help you weigh its merits for your specific business needs.

Strengths:

- The Bowtie / Data Funnel model helps companies understand their customers' journey and identify opportunities to improve the sales process.

- The model provides a comprehensive view of the sales process, from initial awareness to customer retention and expansion.

- Companies can use the Bowtie model to identify areas where they can improve their sales and marketing efforts and provide more value to their customers.

Weaknesses:

- The Bowtie / Data Funnel model can be complicated to implement for companies with limited resources or without a clear understanding of their customers' journey.

- The model is not a one-size-fits-all solution and needs to be tailored to the specific needs of each company.

Summary:

The Bowtie Funnel is a valuable tool for B2B companies looking to optimize their sales and marketing efforts. It provides a comprehensive view of the sales process and helps companies identify opportunities for improvement. By understanding the customer journey, companies can create a more engaging and effective sales process that leads to increased customer retention and revenue growth. However, it's important to tailor the model to the specific needs of each company and invest the necessary resources to make it work effectively.

Chapter 7: Business Stage - Finding the Right Funnel for Your Journey

Throughout our exploration of the various marketing funnels, we've discovered that no single funnel is perfect. Each funnel has its strengths and weaknesses, and choosing the right one for your business depends on your current stage of growth. In this final chapter, we will bring everything together and demonstrate the importance of selecting the appropriate marketing funnel for your business stage. As you master one type of funnel, you can then expand into incorporating additional marketing funnels, such as growth loops and flywheels.

Understanding Your Business Stage

Before diving into the application of different marketing funnels, it's essential to understand the three primary business stages:

- Product-Market Fit
- Go-to-Market Fit
- Scale-Up

Let's take a closer look at each stage and provide examples of successful B2B companies that have leveraged the right marketing funnels for their growth.

Product-Market Fit

At the product-market fit stage, your primary focus is on validating your product or service and ensuring that it meets the needs of your target market. During this stage, your marketing efforts should be centered around the following:

- Identifying your target audience
- Refining your product/service offering
- Testing and iterating on your marketing messages

For businesses in the product-market fit stage, the AIDA Funnel Model can be an effective tool for optimizing marketing efforts. The AIDA model helps you generate awareness, capture interest, create desire, and drive action, which are crucial elements in validating your product and finding the right audience.

Example: A B2B software company in its early stages leverages the AIDA funnel to attract and engage potential customers, refining their messaging based on the feedback received, ultimately achieving product-market fit.

Go-to-Market Fit

Once you've achieved product-market fit, the next stage is go-to-market fit. This stage is all about expanding your reach and generating consistent, predictable growth. During this stage, your marketing efforts should focus on:

- Scaling your marketing channels
- Optimizing your customer acquisition process
- Measuring and tracking your marketing performance

For businesses in the go-to-market fit stage, the AAARR (Pirate Funnel) Framework is an excellent choice. This framework helps you systematically address each stage of the customer journey, from awareness to retention. It allows you to optimize your marketing efforts, ensuring that you are consistently attracting, acquiring, and retaining customers.

Example: A B2B marketing agency that has found product-market fit begins to implement the AAARR framework to expand their reach, optimize their acquisition process, and measure their marketing performance. By doing so, they achieve consistent, predictable growth.

Scale-Up

When your business reaches the scale-up stage, the focus shifts to maximizing growth, expanding market share, and increasing revenue. At this stage, your marketing efforts should concentrate on:

- Expanding into new markets
- Building and nurturing customer relationships

  Leveraging data to optimize and personalize marketing efforts

For businesses in the scale-up stage, the Bowtie/Data Funnel and Growth Loops are powerful tools. The Bowtie/Data Funnel helps you maximize revenue and customer lifetime value by identifying opportunities to upsell, cross-sell, and create recurring revenue. Growth Loops, on the other hand, enable you to build a self-sustaining system that continuously attracts and retains customers, fueling exponential growth.

Example: A B2B SaaS company in the scale-up stage begins to incorporate the Bowtie/Data Funnel and Growth Loops into their marketing strategy. By focusing on customer retention, expansion, and creating a self-sustaining system, they achieve rapid growth and increased market share.

Key Takeaways

As we've explored throughout this ebook, there is no one-size-fits-all solution when it comes to marketing funnels. The key is to understand your business stage and choose the appropriate funnel that best aligns with your goals and objectives. Here are the key takeaways from this chapter:

- Recognize your business stage: Product-Market Fit, Go-to-Market Fit, or Scale-Up
- Choose the right funnel for your stage:
- Product-Market Fit: AIDA Funnel Model
- Go-to-Market Fit: AAARR (Pirate Funnel) Framework
- Scale-Up: Bowtie/Data Funnel and Growth Loops
- Continuously evolve and adapt your marketing strategy to meet the changing needs of your customers and business

By understanding your business stage and selecting the right marketing funnel, you can maximize the effectiveness of your marketing efforts and drive sustainable growth.

Conclusion

The journey through the history and evolution of marketing funnels has been a fascinating one. We've uncovered the strengths and weaknesses of various funnels and demonstrated that no single funnel is perfect. The key to successful marketing lies in understanding your business stage and choosing the appropriate funnel that aligns with your growth objectives.

As you progress through the stages of your business, you may find it necessary to incorporate additional marketing funnels or adapt existing ones to meet the changing needs of your customers and market. By staying agile and responsive to these changes, you can ensure the continued success of your marketing efforts and drive long-term, sustainable growth for your business.

I hope that this ebook has provided you with valuable insights and inspiration for your marketing journey. Remember, the key to success lies in continuously adapting and evolving your marketing strategy to meet the needs of your customers and stay ahead of the competition. I wish you the best of luck on your marketing adventure!

References & Resources

Akgün, V. Ö., & Arslan, B. N. Marketing Mentality of the Modern Age:
Digital Marketing. Available at:
https://www.researchgate.net/profile/V-Oezlem-Akguen/publication/366894201_Marketing_Me
ntality_of_the_Modern_Age_Digital_Marketing/links/63b6f03bc3c99660ebcf6c25/Marketing-M
entality-of-the-Modern-Age-Digital-Marketing.pdf

Banerjee, Madhumita, Is AIDA Effective Tool in Measuring Advertising/Marketing Campaigns? A
Literature Review (October 29, 2022). Available at
SSRN: https://ssrn.com/abstract=4261303

Brian Balfour, C. W. (n.d.). Growth Loops are the New Funnels. From Reforge:
https://www.reforge.com/blog/growth-loops

Chakraborti, T. Electronic Word of Mouth (e-WoM)–Most Powerful Advertisement for Quality
Products. Available at:
https://www.researchgate.net/profile/Drtapas-Chakraborti/publication/348687015_Electronic_
Word_of_Mouth_e-WoM_-Most_Powerful_Advertisement_for_Quality_Products/links/600ae21a9
2851c13fe2b26b6/Electronic-Word-of-Mouth-e-WoM-Most-Powerful-Advertisement-for-Qualit
y-Products.pdf

Choski, N. (2016, June 1). The Revenue Funnel Gets Fancy: Bring On The Bow Tie. From Adobe:
https://blog.adobe.com/en/publish/2016/01/06/the-revenue-funnel-gets-fancybring-on-the-bo
w-tie

Copley, P. (2015, November). For the love of AIDA–developing the Hierarchy of Effects model in
SME social media marketing strategy. In Institute Small Business and Entrepreneurship (ISBE)
Conference, Glasgow, 11th–12th November. Available at:
https://nrl.northumbria.ac.uk/25103/1/Copley%20-%20For%20the%20love%20of%20AIDA.docx

Distel, A. (2022, January 7). How AIDA Marketing Works (and How to Make It Work For You). From Jasper Blog: https://www.jasper.ai/blog/aida-marketing

Dumortier, G. (2022, June 29). Growth Loops: How to Build Marketing Directly Into Your Product. From LinkedIn: https://www.linkedin.com/pulse/growth-loops-how-build-marketing-directly-your-guillaume-dumortier/

Edelman, D. C. (2010). Branding in the digital age. Harvard business review, 88(12), 62-69. Available at: https://depositioneerders.nl/wp-content/uploads/2017/01/Branding-in-the-Digital-Age-HBR.pdf

Frank V. Cespedes, T. B. (2015, August 5). What Salespeople Need to Know About the New B2B Landscape. From Harvard Business Review: https://hbr.org/2015/08/what-salespeople-need-to-know-about-the-new-b2b-landscape
Ginoski, Z. (2019, August 27). The AIDA Model: A Proven Formula For Converting Strangers Into Customers. From LinkedIn: https://www.linkedin.com/pulse/aida-model-zlatko-ginoski/

Growth Loops – The New Way To Grow Bank Product Sales. (2022, May 4). From LinkedIn: https://www.linkedin.com/pulse/growth-loops-new-way-grow-bank-product-sales-chris-nichols/?trk=articles_directory

Halligan, B. (2018, November 20). Replacing the Sales Funnel with the Sales Flywheel. From Harvard Business Review: https://hbr.org/2018/11/replacing-the-sales-funnel-with-the-sales-flywheel

Hamilton, R., & Price, L. L. (2019). Consumer journeys: Developing consumer-based strategy. Journal of the Academy of Marketing Science, 47, 187-191. Available at: https://link.springer.com/article/10.1007/s11747-019-00636-y

Jacob Ader, K. R. (2021, February 12). Why every business needs a full-funnel marketing strategy. From McKinsey & Company: https://www.mckinsey.com/capabilities/growth-marketing-and-sales/our-insights/why-every-business-needs-a-full-funnel-marketing-strategy

Jaura, G. S., & Sharma, T. (2023). A Study on Recent Marketing Trends. Eduzone: International Peer Reviewed/Refereed Multidisciplinary Journal, 12(1), 1-10. Available at: https://www.eduzonejournal.com/index.php/eiprmj/article/view/219

Jerath, K., Ma, L., & Park, Y. H. (2014). Consumer click behavior at a search engine: The role of keyword popularity. Journal of Marketing Research, 51(4), 480-486. Available at: https://journals.sagepub.com/doi/abs/10.1509/jmr.13.0099?journalCode=mrja

Lieberman, M. (2019). How 'the new customer buyer's journey'is reshaping the way you strategically manage your brand. Journal of Brand Strategy, 8(1), 76-85. Available at: https://www.ingentaconnect.com/content/hsp/jbs/2019/00000008/00000001/art00009

Malhotra, G. (2019, April 22). Marketing Bow-Tie vs. Marketing Funnel: How to Impact Revenue with Data Visualization. From LinkedIn: https://www.linkedin.com/pulse/marketing-bow-tie-vs-funnel-how-impact-revenue-data-gary-malhotra/

Mohr, T. (2017, August 2). Scaling the Revenue Engine — Chapter 18: Top of Funnel. From Medium: https://medium.com/ceoquest/scaling-the-revenue-engine-chapter-18-top-of-funnel-6b9f51dbc1d

Nizami, S. (2019). Why growth companies are adopting the flywheel over the marketing funnel. CMO Innovation. Available at: https://www.hubspot.com/flywheel#:~:text=Companies%20that%20choose%20to%20use,customers%20and%20retain%20existing%20ones.

OVERVIEW: AIDA. (n.d.). From Oxford Reference:
https://www.oxfordreference.com/display/10.1093/oi/authority.20110803095432783;jsessionid
=2AB8EE5A6F84073FAFB952F0CC853FD4

Persofsky, Julie & Vanderkooij, Jacco. (2021). CUSTOMER SUCCESS AS A PROFIT CENTER.
Available at:
https://www.researchgate.net/publication/350357210_CUSTOMER_SUCCESS_AS_A_PROFIT_C
ENTER

Polk, X. L. (2018). Marketing: The Key to Successful Teaching and Learning. Journal of
Marketing Development & Competitiveness, 12(2). Available at:
https://www.researchgate.net/profile/Xanshunta-Polk-2/publication/344417647_Marketing_The
_Key_to_Successful_Teaching_and_Learning/links/5f737388458515b7cf585c73/Marketing-The-
Key-to-Successful-Teaching-and-Learning.pdf

PURCĂREA, I. M. Digital Customers, Digital Marketers, and Keeping up with Trends in Today's
Digital World. Available at:
https://www.researchgate.net/profile/Ioan-Matei-Purcarea/publication/343162839_Digital_Cust
omers_Digital_Marketers_and_Keeping_up_with_Trends_in_Today's_Digital_World/links/5f19a43
792851cd5fa3f5f1e/Digital-Customers-Digital-Marketers-and-Keeping-up-with-Trends-in-Toda
ys-Digital-World.pdf

Ratcliffe, J. (2017). Developing metrics for your sales funnel: how to implement the AARRR
acronym. Journal of Aesthetic Nursing, 6(6), 318-319. Available at:
https://www.magonlinelibrary.com/doi/abs/10.12968/joan.2017.6.6.318

Redien-Collot, R. (2022). Growth Loops: From Perceptions of Growth to Motivations for Growth
in High-Growth Women-Led Entrepreneurial Firms. Strategic Entrepreneurship: Perspectives on
Dynamics, Theories, and Practices, 273-301. Available at:
https://link.springer.com/chapter/10.1007/978-3-030-86032-5_13

Sapian, A., & Vyshnevska, M. (2019). The marketing funnel as an effective way of a business strategy. ΛΌΓΟΣ. The art of scientific mind. Available at: https://er.knutd.edu.ua/bitstream/123456789/14560/3/Sapian_A_Vyshnevska_M.pdf

Sharma, S. (2019, March 19). Understanding the Marketing Funnel – What is the Marketing Funnel, how does it work and where can you use it? From LinkedIn: https://www.linkedin.com/pulse/understanding-marketing-funnel-what-how-does-work-where -sharma/

Stareva, I. (2018, September 19). The Funnel is Dead. Long Live the Flywheel! From Medium : https://medium.com/@IliyanaStareva/the-funnel-is-dead-long-live-the-flywheel-e9d6c75248e 4

Team, A. C. (2022, August 29). Learn about the sales funnel and how to optimize it for the best results. From Adobe: https://business.adobe.com/blog/basics/what-is-sales-funnel

Team, A. E. (2022, July 22). Marketing Funnel: How to Build and Create a Successful One. From Adobe: https://business.adobe.com/blog/basics/marketing-funnel

Team, I. E. (2023, March 20). The five marketing funnel stages that are important to know. From Indeed: https://uk.indeed.com/career-advice/career-development/marketing-funnel-stages

TOUHILL, D. (2022, December 13). MARKETING & SALES: The Ultimate Guide to Building a Marketing Funnel. From LEADERS: https://leaders.com/articles/growth/marketing-funnel/

Ullal, M. S., & Hawaldar, I. T. (2018). Influence of advertisement on customers based on AIDA model. Problems and Prospective in Management (December, 2018) Vol, 16(4), 285-298. Available at: https://www.ceeol.com/search/article-detail?id=722919

Van Gasteren, W. (2022). What is the Pirate Funnel (AARRR framework) and how to apply it in 5 quick steps. Available at: https://growwithward.com/aaarrr-pirate-funnel/

Walgrove, A. (n.d.). How marketing funnels work. From Canva: https://www.canva.com/learn/how-marketing-funnels-work/

Thanks For Reading